GRAVITY

Investigating the Force, Mass, and Attraction of Physical Bodies

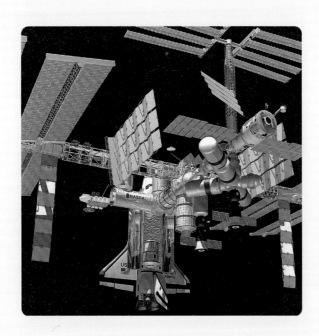

CHRIS WOODFORD

rosen publishing's
rosen
central

New York

This edition first published in 2013 by:

The Rosen Publishing Group, Inc.
29 East 21st Street
New York, NY 10010

Consultant: Don Franceschetti, Ph.D., Distinguished
  Service Professor, Departments of Physics and
  Chemistry, The University of Memphis, Memphis,
  Tennessee

Creative Director: Jeni Child
Picture Researcher: Helen Simm
Illustrators: Darren Awuah,
  Richard Burgess, and Mark Walker
Managing Editor: Tim Harris
Children's Publisher: Anne O'Daly
Production Director: Alastair Gourlay
Editorial Director: Lindsey Lowe

Library of Congress Cataloging-in-Publication Data

Woodford, Chris.
Gravity: investigating the force, mass, and attraction of physical bodies/Chris Woodford.—1st ed.
p. cm.—(Scientific pathways)
Includes bibliographical references and index.
ISBN 978-1-4488-7201-5 (library binding)
1. Gravitation—Juvenile literature. 2. Gravity—Juvenile literature. I. Title.
QC178.W664 2013
531'.14—dc23

2011047885

Manufactured in the United States of America

CPSIA Compliance Information: Batch #S12YA: For further information, contact Rosen Publishing, New York, New York, at 1-800-237-9932.

CONTENTS

INTRODUCTION

Gravity is like glue that holds the universe together. This invisible force that makes objects fall to Earth also keeps the stars and planets circling in continuous cosmic movement.

GRAVITY IS EVERYWHERE. IT IS gravity that pulls a ball back down to Earth when it is thrown into the air. It is gravity that makes a stone feel heavy and a feather feel light. Gravity drags ocean tides back and forth and keeps people from flying off Earth as the planet spins on its axis. Gravity also makes the planets orbit the Sun.

From the Sun to the Moon and from gigantic boulders to tiny specks of dust, every object in the universe attracts every other object with the invisible force called gravity (or gravitational force). Heavier objects have more mass, so they exert a bigger force of gravity than lighter objects, which have less mass. Gravity works a bit like magnetism, another invisible force. Magnets can either pull (attract) or push (repel) other objects, but gravity is always a pulling force.

Magnetism is a very powerful force over short distances—strong magnets can lift cars or even trucks. Gravity, on the other hand, is a much weaker force, but it can act over an infinite distance. Earth is 93 million miles (150 million km) from the Sun. Yet the gravitational force between them is strong enough to keep our massive planet revolving in orbit around the Sun rather than flying off into space.

Gravity has controlled the development of the universe since the time of the big bang, the moment when the universe began, some 13 or 14 billion years ago. Gravity will also determine exactly how and when the universe will end.

Despite gravity's importance, people have started to understand it only in the last three hundred years or so. Before the seventeenth century, astronomers (people who study the sky) had little idea what kept the planets in orbit and no idea that it was the same force that made objects fall to Earth. How the mysteries of gravity have been discovered and gradually understood is a fascinating story that has challenged some of the greatest scientific minds of all time.

1 EARLY OBSERVATIONS

Ancient peoples knew nothing about gravity. They watched the heavens regularly, but they understood little of how or why the stars and planets moved as they did.

IN THE BRIGHTLY LIT CITIES of the modern world, few people notice—let alone observe—the night sky. Things were very different for ancient peoples who lived around three thousand to six thousand years ago. To these first astronomers, the sky was an important source of knowledge. The planets and stars gave people the information they needed to figure out

PLANETS AND STARS

Planets, like Earth and Venus (right), are massive objects that move through the heavens. They do not give off light, but glow brightly with reflected light from the Sun. The Sun is a star, not a planet. Stars are glowing balls of gas held together by gravity. Like fires, candles, and other hot objects, stars give off their own light. The movements of planets and stars are controlled by gravity.

INDIAN IDEAS

Animals played a role in the ideas that India's ancient Hindus had about the universe. Ancient Hindus thought the world rested on four elephants, which stood on a huge tortoise, which in turn balanced on a gigantic serpent.

ECLIPSES

During a full eclipse of the Sun (a solar eclipse), the Moon moves between Earth and the Sun, which plunges parts of Earth briefly into total darkness. In an eclipse of the Moon (a lunar eclipse), the Earth's shadow falls across part or all of the visible surface of the Moon.

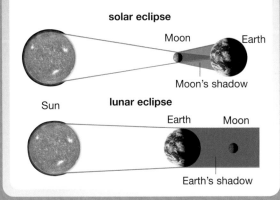

time, to create calendars, and to plan their lives. How the sky worked was a mystery, although the ancients came up with many ideas to explain what they saw.

In India, ancient priests suggested that the world was built on huge stone pillars. This explained why it was dark at night—the Sun moved back under the world, between the pillars, so it was in the right place to rise on the other side the next morning.

Without the knowledge of gravity to explain the science of the sky, ancient astronomers had to rely on imagination. In China, astronomers were able to make careful observations of the stars more than four thousand years ago. They could even predict the timing of the next solar eclipse,

This map of the twelve astrological constellations was published in 1661.

ASTROLOGERS

The Babylonians developed astrology around 400 BCE. Astrology is based on the idea that the movements of planets and stars influence a person's life. The demand for accurate horoscopes (forecasts drawn up by astrologers) made the Babylonians watch the skies closely. Astrology is not scientific, unlike astronomy, and modern astronomers view it with a great deal of skepticism.

VENUS TABLET

The Venus Tablet (below) dates from the reign of Babylonian king Hammurabi (1792–1750 BCE). It is made of clay and contains markings in an ancient script called cuneiform. The tablet made predictions about Earth's weather based on when and where Venus appeared in the night sky, and what the planet looked like.

although they believed the Sun disappeared because a huge dragon was trying to eat it.

We know ancient civilizations practiced astronomy because some of the records they kept still survive. In Babylon (an ancient settlement near the modern city of Baghdad in Iraq), astrologers kept records on clay tablets. The oldest of these is called the Venus Tablet.

By around 350 BCE, the Babylonians had developed mathematics that was sophisticated enough to help them predict accurately the movements of the planets and the arrival of eclipses. Watching the skies also allowed the Babylonians to develop a calendar. At around the same time, the ancient Egyptians developed their own calendar that featured the 24-hour day and 365-day year that we still use today. An accurate calendar was essential in Egypt, where planting and harvesting crops had to be carefully timed around the annual flood of the Nile River.

Ancient civilizations such as those of the Chinese, the Babylonians, and the Egyptians played an important part in the early days of astronomy. Their people were the first to watch the skies, track the movements of planets, and predict events such as eclipses. None of these ancient peoples, though, really developed scientific theories of how or why the universe worked as it did. They had no idea that the things they saw in the skies above them were controlled by the force of gravity.

ANCIENT CALENDARS

Ancient civilizations needed accurate calendars, which had to be calculated from the movements of the planets. The Babylonian calendar used twelve equal months of twenty-eight days, based on the cycle of the Moon. Extra months had to be added every two or three years to make the calendar work properly. The Egyptian year consisted of twelve months of thirty days, with five extra days added at the end of each year to correct the calendar.

The Great Pyramid of Cheops at Giza was used as an astronomical observatory by ancient Egyptian priests.

2 THE SCIENTIFIC METHOD

In ancient times, curiosity about the skies led to scientific theories about the workings of the universe. The quest that would eventually lead to gravity began with ancient thinkers such as Aristotle, Pythagoras, and Ptolemy.

THE ANCIENT GREEKS WERE the first people to question why the heavens moved as they did. Earlier civilizations, such as the Babylonians and Egyptians, had gathered knowledge simply to help with practical problems, such as developing calendars. The Greek philosophers, however, pursued

ANCIENT GREECE

From literature to music, from architecture to sport, and from art to religion, the ancient Greeks laid the foundations of the western world. Their civilization flourished in the southern European country of Greece between around 600 BCE and 200 BCE.

This ancient Greek vase shows the sport of wrestling.

PHILOSOPHERS AND PHILOSOPHY

Philosophers are people who think logically about problems such as why the world exists and how people should gather knowledge about things. Astronomy was one of the chief concerns of Greek philosophers, who combined their talent for reasoning with their skills in mathematics to develop the first scientific theories.

This eighteenth-century painting shows philosophers deep in discussion.

knowledge for its own sake in an attempt to understand what caused the stars and planets to move.

The ancient Greeks devised theories about the world that

INDUCTION AND DEDUCTION

Scientists come up with theories based on careful observations of what they have seen. If they think up a general theory about something based on observations and other facts, that is called induction. An example of induction is: Earth is probably round because ships disappear over the horizon. Once they have thought up a general theory, scientists can try to figure out other things that follow from it. That is called deduction, which means figuring out specific conclusions from a general theory. An example of deduction is: All planets go around the Sun. Earth is a planet. Therefore Earth goes around the Sun.

The Greeks used induction and deduction but generally did not test their theories by experiment.

THEORIES

A scientific theory does two things: It *explains* what scientists have already seen and it *predicts* what they might see in the future. The predictions that follow from a theory enable scientists to test whether the theory is correct and to develop better theories. The process of developing and testing theories is known as the scientific method.

One of the most famous Greek thinkers was Aristotle (384–322 BCE). He developed some of the first theories about how the universe works.

could be tested by observation. This almost made them the first scientists. Like scientists today, the Greeks used two types of thinking, induction and deduction, in developing their theories.

THE FIRST SCIENTIST?

Thales (625–546 BCE), who was born in Miletus in Asia Minor (what is now Turkey), was perhaps one of the world's first scientists. Not satisfied with explanations based on myths or stories about gods and monsters, Thales tried to understand in a scientific way why things really happened.

Many thinkers contributed to the ancient Greeks' knowledge about the world. The first was probably Thales of Miletus, who suggested Earth was a flat disk that floated on water, a substance from which he believed everything was made. A student of Thales, mathematician and astronomer Anaximander, thought everything evolved from an infinite, invisible substance that he called "apeiron" (the boundless).

Later Greek thinkers built on these ideas. In the fifth century BCE, Pythagoras and his followers argued that Earth was a globe that revolved with the Sun and the other planets around a fire. A more advanced version of this idea was put forward by a philosopher called Aristotle

ANAXIMANDER'S UNIVERSE

Anaximander (c. 610–546 BCE; left), who invented mapmaking, also wrote an early explanation of the cosmos. He thought the universe was made up of huge cylinders that whirled around inside one another. The Sun was on the outer cylinder. Next came the Moon, then the stars, and finally Earth, on the inside.

(384—322 BCE) in his book *On the Heavens*. Aristotle was one of the first people to think about gravity. He believed (wrongly) that heavy objects fall faster than light ones. He thought this was because heavy objects moved naturally toward the center of Earth. He also believed that the planets moved naturally around the heavens without the help of any kind of force.

What Aristotle did not realize was that these things were connected. The modern concept of gravity explains both the way that objects fall toward Earth and the way the planets move through the heavens.

ON THE HEAVENS

Aristotle's book *On the Heavens* was written around 340 BCE and describes a universe in which the Sun, Moon, stars, and planets revolve in circular paths around a fixed Earth. Aristotle observed that Earth cast a round shadow on the Moon during an eclipse and realized that Earth must be a sphere rather than a flat disk.

Earth casts a curved shadow on the Moon during an eclipse.

MUSICAL PLANETS

Best known for developing trigonometry (the math of triangles), Pythagoras (*c.* 569–*c.* 475 BCE; below) was also an important astronomer. With his followers, the Pythagoreans, he believed the planets were attached to invisible globes that moved around and made a musical sound called "the harmony of the spheres" as they did so.

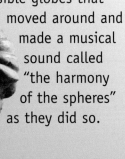

13

THE ALMAGEST

The first encyclopedia of astronomy, Ptolemy's *Almagest* was a thirteen-part book published around 150 CE. It was a digest of everything astronomers had discovered before Ptolemy and had a huge influence on those who came after him. It was based on the observations of an important Greek astronomer called Hipparchus (*c.* 180–*c.* 125 BCE), who had developed the first testable theories of astronomy three hundred years earlier. Ptolemy's book became known as the *Almagest*, which means "the Greatest," when astronomers realized just how important it was.

Ptolemy looks at the stars in an illustration from a book called Margarita Philosophica, *published in the sixteenth century.*

One of the most influential early astronomers was ancient Egyptian mathematician Claudius Ptolemaeus (*c.*100–*c.*170 CE), usually known as Ptolemy. Little is known about Ptolemy's life, but his ideas, collected in an important encyclopedia called the *Almagest*, dominated astronomy for around fourteen hundred years. The *Almagest* was remarkable for many reasons, including its huge catalog of more than a thousand stars. The most important thing about it, though, was its geocentric theory of the universe. This was the first detailed explanation of how the universe worked. Unlike earlier theories, it used complex math to explain and predict the movements of the planets around Earth with considerable accuracy.

GEOCENTRIC THEORY

Ptolemy's geocentric (Earth-centered) theory was based on the idea that the planets revolve in circular paths around Earth, which is fixed at the center of the universe. According to Ptolemy, Earth is spherical, not flat, and sits in the middle of a set of concentric spheres. These are increasingly large spheres with a common center (a bit like the layers of an onion) and mark the paths on which the Moon, the Sun, the planets, and stars circle around Earth.

A geocentric armillary sphere from 1554 with Earth at the center. The surrounding rings show the paths of the planets and stars.

With Ptolemy's *Almagest*, astronomy became a truly sophisticated science based on mathematics and reason.

After the end of the ancient Greek civilization and the Roman Empire that conquered the Greeks, science and culture developed much more slowly in Europe in a period known as the Middle Ages (*c.* 500–*c.*1500 CE) Many ideas developed by the Greeks and Romans were lost during this time and had to be rediscovered later. The astronomical theories of Ptolemy and the ancient Greeks were preserved in the Islamic world, though, by scholars such as Hypatia and mathematician al-Khwarizmi (*c.* 780–*c.*850 CE) Islamic knowledge trickled back to Europe toward the end of the Middle Ages.

HYPATIA

Widely regarded as the first great woman scientist, Hypatia (*c.* 370–*c.*415 CE) was a professor of philosophy, mathematics, and astronomy in the Egyptian city of Alexandria. She was a great speaker who was also known for her beauty. When she became caught up in a religious conflict, she was murdered by a mob of angry monks (left).

3 GREAT CONTROVERSIES

When Renaissance astronomers suggested that the planets revolved around the Sun, it marked the beginning of a deep and sometimes bitter split between science and religion.

PTOLEMY'S IDEA THAT EARTH was at the center of the universe proved popular with astronomers for fourteen hundred years because it explained many phenomena. It was a very intricate theory, however, and not everyone believed that something so complex could be correct. During the Renaissance (see page 18), a Polish astronomer named Nicolaus

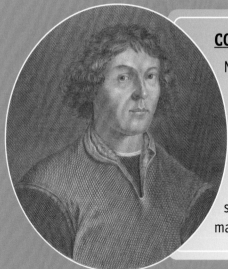

COPERNICUS THE POLYMATH

Nicolaus Copernicus (left; 1473–1543) studied the arts, medicine, law, and church administration before he turned to geography and astronomy. He was a polymath: someone who studies and thinks about many different subjects.

SIMPLY THE BEST

Scientists believe simple theories are more likely to be right than complicated ones. This belief, known as Ockham's Razor after English philosopher William of Ockham (*c.* 1285–1349), explains why people preferred the simpler theory of Copernicus to the complicated one put forward by Ptolemy.

Copernicus proposed a quite different theory of how the universe worked. Copernicus described Ptolemy's complex theory as "a monster." Instead, he revived a simple idea that had been suggested by ancient Greek thinker Aristarchus (c. 310–230 BCE)—Earth and the other planets revolved around the Sun. This is called the heliocentric (Sun-centered) theory.

Copernicus was afraid of publishing the heliocentric theory in case people did not agree with him. At first, the Catholic Church had no problem with the new idea. The pope approved it, and the Catholic Church even used the new theory to create its religious calendar. The Protestants, however, believed that the new theory was both blasphemous and dangerous.

BLASPHEMY

The Copernican theory seemed to go against the Bible, which states that Earth was the center of God's creation. If Earth revolved around the Sun, as Copernicus argued, this seemed to throw into doubt the religious picture of Earth, heaven, and hell described in the Bible. The Protestant reformer Martin Luther (1483–1546) called Copernicus an "upstart astrologer." Others condemned Copernicus's ideas as blasphemous (an insult to God).

This 1708 map depicts Earth at the center of the universe.

BURNED AT THE STAKE

Free thinking and fiery tempered, Italian philosopher Giordano Bruno (*c.* 1548–1600) was good at upsetting people. During the 1560s, he was accused of heresy (arguing against the church).

In 1576 he narrowly escaped being tried for murder. He was not so lucky in 1592, when he was imprisoned for blasphemy and heresy. He refused to apologize and was burned at the stake in 1600.

THE RENAISSANCE

The Renaissance (a word meaning rebirth) was the period of western civilization from roughly 1400 to 1600 CE, when Europe emerged from the Middle Ages. During this time, the old ideas of the ancient Greeks and Romans were rediscovered, and new ideas flourished in art, architecture, and science.

Renaissance astronomers watching an eclipse of the Sun.

The Catholic Church changed its mind and began to criticize Copernicus's theory, too. The theory was eventually published in a book called *De Revolutionibus Orbium Coelestium* (*On the Revolutions of the Celestial Spheres*) in 1543, shortly before Copernicus's death. The publisher of *De Revolutionibus* feared criticism, however, and added a comment to the start of the book. He explained that Copernicus's ideas were designed simply to help with astronomical calculations and the universe did not really work as Copernicus claimed.

Nevertheless, once Copernicus had revived the theory of a heliocentric universe, other astronomers soon began to champion the idea. When another Renaissance thinker, Giordano Bruno, took up the heliocentric theory, it was bad news for both Bruno and the theory. Bruno lost out by supporting what seemed to be blasphemous ideas. The theory suffered by being linked with someone who had always been wildly controversial.

Renaissance thinkers were not all as controversial as Bruno. In 1588, another astronomer, Tycho Brahe, offered a theory more acceptable to the church. He combined Ptolemy's ideas with those of Copernicus. Based on many accurate observations of the skies, Brahe's model of the universe suggested the planets revolved around the Sun, which in turn moved around

OBSERVATIONS

Scientific theories must be based on precise observations of how the world appears to work. Tycho Brahe is best remembered today for making many extremely accurate records of the night sky at a time when telescopes had not yet been invented.

TYCHO BRAHE

The son of a Danish nobleman, Tycho Brahe (1546–1601) was a colorful character. When his nose was sliced off during a duel, he took to wearing a false nose made of silver.

Brahe decided to become an astronomer when, at the age of fourteen, he watched a total eclipse of the Sun. Years later, as a law student, he stayed up at night and watched the stars. He became famous after he spotted a far-off supernova (exploding star) in 1572. This important observation disproved a long-held theory that no change could occur in the heavens beyond the range of the Moon.

Brahe in his observatory at Stjerneborg, Hven, Denmark.

the stationary Earth. It did not explain that the planets moved because of gravity, as scientists now understand.

Brahe's model of the universe still had the Sun circling Earth. When Brahe died in 1601, his assistant Johannes Kepler began to analyze Brahe's astronomical records. Determined to work out a mathematical theory that explained the universe, Kepler came up with three laws. His most important discovery was that Earth and the other planets did indeed go around the Sun. He did not, however, make a connection between his laws and gravity.

Without good scientific instruments, Renaissance astronomers had found it difficult to test their theories. In 1609 Italian mathematician and physicist Galileo Galilei (1564–1642) used the

STRUGGLING TO SEE

German astronomer Johannes Kepler (left; 1571–1630) had very poor eyesight. This was one of the main reasons why it took six long years of study before he finally published his bold new theory, in 1609, in a book called *The New Astronomy*.

KEPLER'S LAWS

The three basic ideas in *The New Astronomy* are known as Kepler's laws. They are:

1) The planets move around the Sun in oval-shaped orbits (paths) called ellipses.
2) Planets move more quickly when they are nearer to the Sun than when they are farther away.
3) The time it takes for a planet to make one orbit is linked to its distance from the Sun.

The Temple of Urania, the muse of astronomy, designed by Kepler.

TELESCOPES

The telescope was invented in 1608 by Dutch eyeglass maker Hans Lippershey (*c.* 1570–1619). When Galileo heard of the idea, he built telescopes of his own. On January 7, 1610, he made his first major observation when he saw the moons of Jupiter.

Galileo's telescope, which he built at the beginning of the seventeenth century.

newly invented telescope to observe the skies. Earlier in his life, he had carried out experiments on gravity.

What Galileo saw through his telescope convinced him that the heliocentric theories of Kepler and Copernicus were correct. Encouraged by astronomers who believed the old geocentric theory, the church accused Galileo of heresy and ordered him not to teach his ideas. When he ignored them and published his theories in 1632, he was arrested and sentenced to life imprisonment. The sentence against him was announced in every university, and his book was burned. Although Galileo experimented on gravity and described how the universe worked, he failed to put these two things together.

EXPERIMENTS ON GRAVITY

Galileo (right) studied gravity by timing how long it took for things to fall when he dropped them, and by rolling balls down slopes so that they would fall more slowly than if they were dropped. He argued that light and heavy objects would fall in exactly the same way in the absence of air resistance. In a vacuum, a feather and a hammer would hit the ground at the same time—a prediction confirmed by Apollo astronauts on the Moon in 1969. In air, the feather takes longer to reach the ground because air resistance slows it down, like a parachute.

4 GRAVITY IS EXPLAINED

Although Kepler's laws showed how Earth and the other planets moved, they did not explain why. That task fell upon English mathematician Isaac Newton and his law of gravitation.

THERE WERE VARIOUS THEORIES about what kept the planets moving around the Sun. Kepler thought that planets were lazy and moved only because the Sun pushed them around. French philosopher René Descartes (1596–1650) believed the planets were pulled around the Sun by suction,

WEIGHT ON OTHER PLANETS

Mass and weight are different things. A person's mass is the amount of matter in their body. Their weight is a measure of how much their mass is attracted by the force of gravity. Unlike their mass, which stays the same, their weight varies. Suppose a person weighs 84 pounds (38 kg) on Earth. On Mars, they would weigh just 31 pounds (14 kg), while on Jupiter they would weigh more than 196 pounds (89 kg)!

MAGNETIC EARTH?

Physicist and physician William Gilbert (left; 1544–1603) was the most distinguished English scientist of his day. He was the first Englishman to support the modern theories of Copernicus. He was also a pioneer in the study of electricity and magnetism. In 1600 Gilbert published an influential book, *De Magnete* (*On Magnetism*), which suggested Earth was a gigantic magnet. Some English scientists believed Earth's magnetism could explain gravity.

ROBERT HOOKE

English physicist Robert Hooke (1635–1703) is best remembered for Hooke's law, which explains how materials behave when they are stretched. His many other contributions to physics include theories of gravity, combustion (how things burn), and kinetic theory (how moving molecules store heat energy).

Robert Hooke was also a microscope pioneer. This is one of his microscopes.

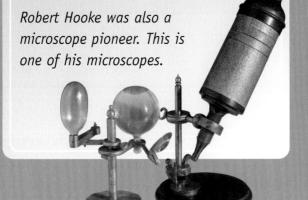

GRAVITATING POWER

In 1674 Robert Hooke wrote the first accurate description of gravity: "All celestial bodies [stars and planets] whatsoever have an attraction or gravitating power toward their own centers, whereby they attract not only their own parts, and keep them from flying from them, as we may observe the Earth to do, but that they do also attract all the other celestial bodies that are within the sphere [influence] of their activity."

like objects being dragged around a whirlpool. English scientists believed the planets were kept in place by some kind of magnetism.

One Englishman who explored this idea was Robert Hooke. Hooke suggested in 1674 that, instead of magnetism, some kind of gravitating power was responsible for the movement of planets. Although he described accurately the idea of gravity as we understand it today, he did not come up with a complete theory. Instead, some five years later, he asked Isaac Newton (1643–1727), a professor of mathematics at England's Cambridge University, to solve the problem of how gravity really worked.

According to legend, it was not complex mathematics that helped

NEWTON THE ALCHEMIST

Alchemy is the idea that ordinary metals can be transformed into gold and that there are special potions (called elixirs) that can extend human life forever. Newton kept very quiet about his experiments in alchemy, which could have destroyed his scientific reputation.

NEWTON'S DISPUTES

Newton (below) once said: "If I have seen farther, it is by standing on the shoulders of giants." Yet he may not have been as modest as he seemed. A private and sensitive man, he was easily offended.

He was anxious about having his ideas published, but he defended them jealously and entered into violent disputes with a number of other scientists who tried to claim credit for similar ideas.

Newton crack the problem of gravity, but an apple falling from a tree. Either way, he arrived at a complete theory of gravity in 1687. The universal law of gravitation, as this is known, is a simple mathematical equation. It shows that all objects in the universe attract one another with a pulling force called gravity. The attraction (pull) between two objects is greater the more massive they are (more mass they have) and the closer they are to one another. Gravity works between objects in both directions at once: Earth not only pulls a falling apple downward but also the apple pulls Earth upward at the same time! The apple's effect on Earth is too slight to measure, however.

Unlike all the astronomers who had come before him, Newton had

HALLEY'S COMET

When English astronomer Edmond Halley (1656–1742) saw a comet in 1682, he realized it was the same one that had appeared in 1531 and 1607. Using the law developed by his friend Isaac Newton, he correctly predicted it would return in 1758.

The comet was later named in Halley's honor. The comet had also appeared in 1066 at the time of the Norman invasion of England. Its appearance was recorded in the eleventh-century Bayeux Tapestry (right).

successfully come up with the first complete theory of gravity. It united what happened on Earth with what happened in space. It described how the planets moved and it explained why they did so.

With his 1687 law of gravitation, Newton not only explained gravity, he also showed how the complex natural world can often be explained by simple and elegant theories. Like all good theories, Newton's law could be used to make predictions. One of Newton's friends, Edmond Halley, used the law to predict correctly when a comet in the sky would return again in the future.

NEWTON AND THE APPLE

As he watched an apple fall toward Earth (right), Newton is supposed to have realized it was being pulled by the very same force that kept the planets moving in their orbits: gravity. Some historians believe Newton invented the apple story himself to suggest that he was a genius.

5 EINSTEIN'S REVELATIONS

Newton's ideas completely changed how people viewed the universe. Around two hundred years later, Albert Einstein's theory of relativity forced people to rethink their ideas about gravity.

NEWTON'S THEORY WAS AN extraordinary achievement. It summed up everything people had discovered about gravity, up to that point in history. Newton's ideas give a good explanation of how most things work on Earth, most of the time. Yet there are some things the laws cannot explain. This became apparent in 1905 with the work of German physicist Albert Einstein. Physicists had for some time been trying to measure the effect

CLASSICAL PHYSICS

In addition to the law of gravitation, Newton also developed three laws of motion, which explain how forces make objects move. Together, Newton's laws are sometimes known as classical physics.

THE NAUGHTY GENIUS

Albert Einstein (right; 1879–1955) first became interested in physics at the age of five, when his father showed him a compass. It intrigued him that the needle always pointed to north and, as he said later, he knew "something deeply hidden had to be behind things." Although he was expelled from one school for disruptive behavior, his brilliant ideas eventually revolutionized the science of the universe.

of Earth's motion on measurements of the speed of light. According to classical physics, during Earth's orbit around the Sun the speed of light from a star ought to appear slightly slower when Earth was moving away from it, and slightly faster when moving toward the star. Such effects were never found.

Einstein decided that the only explanation was if the speed of light through space always had the same value, regardless of the motion of the person measuring it. Einstein then did a number of thought experiments to figure out how objects would have to behave at very high speeds if his theory was true. He found that objects would have an increase in mass while they were moving while their length would appear to decrease. He also found that a moving clock would move more slowly than a stationary one.

THOUGHT EXPERIMENTS

A thought experiment is something you can do in your imagination but not in real life. In one of Einstein's first thought experiments, he imagined what would happen if he sat on a beam of light and watched the world around him. This was one of the experiences that led him to the theory of relativity. Physicists still use thought experiments today. No one knows what happens inside black holes, for example, but with mathematics and thought experiments, scientists can make pretty good guesses.

RELATIVE TIME

In another thought experiment, Einstein imagined what would happen with two twins when one stayed on Earth and the other traveled through space at close to the speed of light. The speed at which the second twin traveled would mean that time would slow for him, so when he returned to Earth, he would be younger than his twin. This has been tested in an experiment in which a highly accurate atomic clock was flown in a jet airplane along a set course while its twin remained stationary. When the flight ended, the moving clock had recorded slightly less elapsed time, just as Einstein predicted.

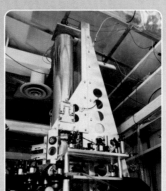

An atomic clock.

27

MASS AND ENERGY

Einstein's famous equation $E=mc^2$ shows that a small amount of mass (matter) can be turned into a huge amount of energy. (In the equation, *E* stands for energy, *m* stands for mass, and *c* stands for the speed of light.) This is the basic idea behind nuclear power and atom bombs (right). It also explains how stars use matter to make their energy.

Einstein's conclusions as to the behavior of objects as seen by observers moving with respect to each other (in relative motion) have become known as the special theory of relativity. One of the most unusual things that follows from this theory is the idea that mass and energy are two different versions of exactly the same thing.

The special theory of relativity said a lot about space, time, and light, but very little about gravity. Gravity is one of the most important theories about the universe, so it needed to be included as well. In 1916, Einstein extended the special theory to cover all of physics, including gravity. He called this more complete explanation the general theory of relativity.

In classical physics, space and time are a bit like a checkerboard. Newton's laws said that gravity

EINSTEIN AND NEWTON

Einstein greatly admired Newton, without whose earlier work the theory of relativity would have been impossible. Both men believed in an orderly universe that worked in a predictable way. Einstein once said, "God does not play dice." He meant he did not believe that the universe could be random or chaotic.

was a mysterious invisible force, like magnetism, that pulled objects toward one another across the board.

In Einstein's general theory, the space time checkerboard behaves like a sheet of thin rubber. When a heavy object is placed on the rubber, it bends it downward. This makes other objects roll downhill toward it as though a force (gravity) were pulling them together. According to Einstein, gravity is not a force but a bending of space and time by mass. The effects of gravity are the same as—or equivalent to—those of acceleration.

SPACE TIME

For Newton, the three dimensions of space were completely separate from time. In his general theory of relativity, Einstein suggested that space and time were linked together to make a four-dimensional structure called space time, or the space time continuum.

The space time checkerboard (1) is warped by huge objects such as stars (2). This effect is what we call gravity.

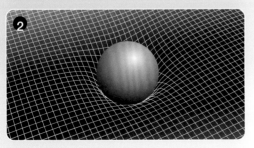

EQUIVALENCE

Einstein explained gravity in a way unlike anyone before him. Suppose an astronaut in a spacecraft drops a pen. If the spacecraft were parked on its launchpad on Earth, the pen would fall toward the floor because of Earth's gravity. If the spacecraft were in deep space and accelerating (increasing its speed), though, the pen might be seen as floating in midair, with the floor of the spacecraft moving up toward it. Einstein called this idea equivalence. It means that gravity and acceleration can produce exactly the same effect—the "falling" pen.

6 THE BIG BANG AND AN EXPANDING UNIVERSE

All scientific theories need proof of some kind if people are to believe them. Einstein's ideas about gravity were so extraordinary that the need for convincing proof was especially important.

WHEN EINSTEIN WAS AWARDED the prestigious Nobel Prize in 1921, it was not for the theory of relativity but for his other work in physics.

The theory of relativity was too controversial and remained open to debate. Parts of the theory had been proved during a solar eclipse

THE 1919 ECLIPSE

Einstein's general theory of relativity suggested stars near the Sun would appear to be in slightly the wrong positions, because the light rays they sent out would be bent by the Sun's mass. During a solar eclipse in 1919, British physicist Arthur Stanley Eddington (1882–1944) saw that this really happened. Einstein immediately became world famous, because an important part of his theory had been proved correct.

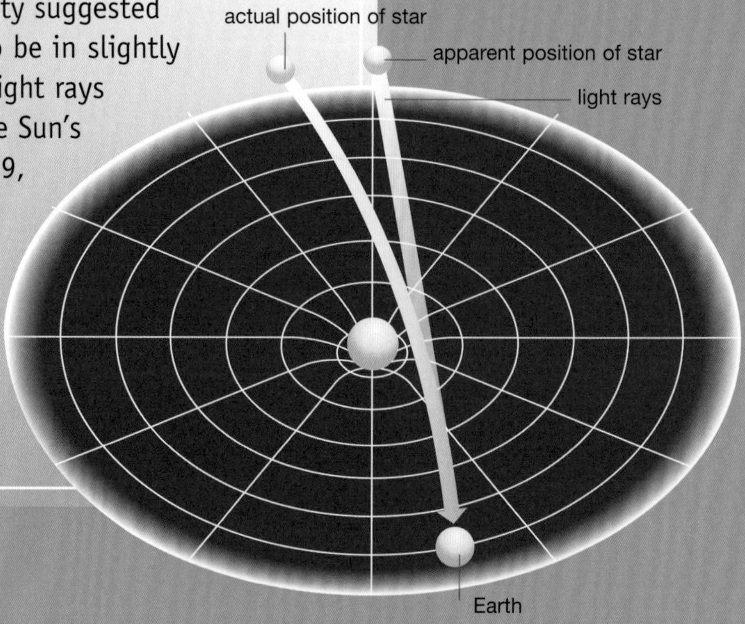

actual position of star
apparent position of star
light rays
Earth

in 1919 and by predictions about Mercury's orbit. Einstein had been acclaimed as one of the greatest scientific geniuses of all time, yet few people really understood his theories or how they explained gravity. Like any scientific theory, Einstein's theory of relativity needed to be tested.

One of the most dramatic things that follows from Einstein's theory is the idea that the universe is either expanding or contracting. Einstein was not sure whether to believe this, and he could not test it, so he changed his theory instead. He suggested that there is a force that pushes galaxies apart and balances the force of gravity that pulls them together. The net result is a static universe that is neither expanding nor contracting.

Mercury's orbit

Sun

Mercury's perihelion

Mercury

MERCURY'S PERIHELION

Before Einstein, astronomers had never been able to explain an unusual fact about Mercury's orbit. The perihelion of a planet is the point in its orbit when the planet passes closest to the Sun. For planets not so close to the Sun, the perihelion is always at the same point in space, but for Mercury the perihelion moves about the Sun very slowly over the course of many years. The first proof of Einstein's theories was that they predicted Mercury's movements exactly.

HUBBLE AND THE BIG BANG

In 1929 American astronomer Edwin Hubble (1889–1953), for whom the Hubble telescope is named, proved that the universe is expanding like the surface of a balloon does as it is being inflated. This suggested there was once a time when the universe was infinitely small, and led to the theory that it was created at a definite time called the big bang. Hubble (below; right) is seen here receiving an award for his work on space research.

BLACK HOLES

Although black holes were first suggested in 1783 by English physicist John Michell (1724–1793), the mathematics in Einstein's general theory of relativity confirmed that they could really exist.

This galaxy is thought to contain a black hole at its center.

In 1929 American astronomer Edwin Hubble discovered that distant galaxies are moving away from Earth in all directions. This meant the universe was definitely expanding. Einstein had been wrong about the static universe. He described this as "the biggest mistake of my life."

Another prediction that follows from Einstein's general theory is the idea that there are black holes in space. Formed when stars collapse, black holes are massive and dense and have such a strong gravitational pull that even light cannot escape from them. Astronomers using the Hubble telescope have found some evidence of black holes, but no one has yet found absolute proof of their existence.

NO ESCAPE?

Stephen Hawking has suggested that "black holes ain't so black." The fact that light cannot escape from black holes gives them their name. Hawking believes, though, that black holes may give off particles of other radiation and glow, just like hot objects do. Eventually, black holes vanish completely in a huge explosion equivalent to that of millions of nuclear bombs.

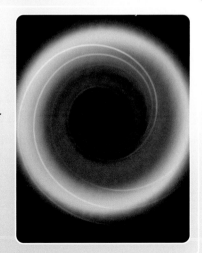

An illustration of gas from a star being drawn by gravity into a black hole in a swirling pattern.

One of the world's leading experts on black holes, Stephen Hawking, believes there may be more black holes in the universe than visible stars. He thinks the huge gravitational pull these black holes exert may explain why our galaxy rotates as it does. Hawking also believes that there may be a gigantic black hole at the center of our universe. The work of such scientists as Hubble and Hawking has given important support to Einstein's general theory of relativity. It is still far from a complete explanation of gravity, but it is a step closer to that goal.

STEPHEN HAWKING

Stephen Hawking (right) was born in 1942, three hundred years after Galileo's death. Confined to a wheelchair by the muscle-wasting disorder amyotrophic lateral sclerosis, Hawking is unable to speak without help and delivers his lectures using a computer voice synthesizer. Until 2009 Hawking was Lucasian Professor of Mathematics at England's Cambridge University, a position once held by Isaac Newton (*see* pages 22–25).

7 FUTURE PROSPECTS

Could all of physics, including gravity, soon be explained by a single theory? Or will new discoveries force physicists to rethink their ideas completely?

EINSTEIN'S THEORY OF relativity was one of the two greatest theories of physics of the twentieth century. The other was quantum mechanics. While relativity explains the large-scale, cosmic world of stars, galaxies, and black holes, quantum mechanics explains the extremely

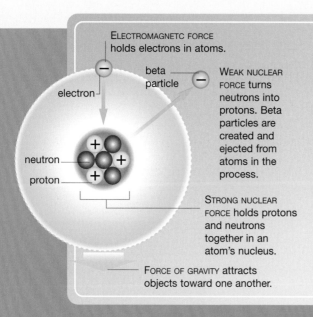

ELECTROMAGNETC FORCE holds electrons in atoms.

electron

beta particle

WEAK NUCLEAR FORCE turns neutrons into protons. Beta particles are created and ejected from atoms in the process.

neutron

proton

STRONG NUCLEAR FORCE holds protons and neutrons together in an atom's nucleus.

FORCE OF GRAVITY attracts objects toward one another.

THE THEORY OF EVERYTHING

The entire universe seems to be controlled by just four forces (left). These are the strong nuclear force that holds atoms together, the weak nuclear force that controls radioactivity, the electromagnetic force responsible for electricity and magnetism, and gravity. Physicists have so far managed to combine the first three of these forces in a single theory. They have yet to decide where gravity fits.

GRAVITONS

Quantum theory suggests that two particles can attract one another by swapping another particle in a sort of subatomic game of catch. This binds the particles together as though a force acted between them. Gravity is caused when particles throw and catch a different kind of particle called a graviton.

small-scale subatomic world—the mini-universe inside the atom.

Physicists are now trying to combine relativity and quantum mechanics into a single theory called quantum gravity. This ambitious project could eventually lead to a "theory of everything." It would unite and explain the four fundamental forces that are believed to control the universe, it would explain how things work on both the cosmic and subatomic scale, and it would explain both the beginning of the universe and how it will end.

According to quantum gravity, the force of gravity is carried by particles called gravitons, which travel at the speed of light. The gravitational pull that keeps Earth revolving around the Sun is really a stream of tiny,

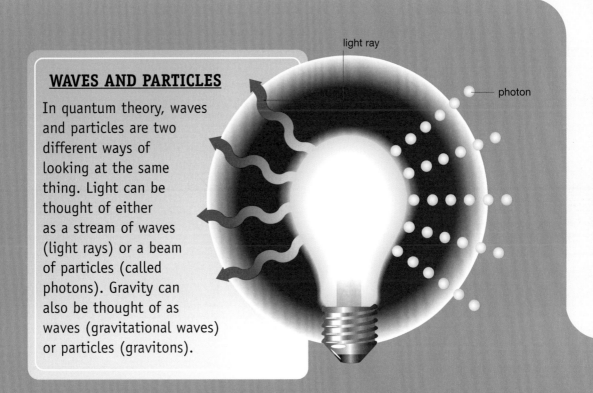

WAVES AND PARTICLES

In quantum theory, waves and particles are two different ways of looking at the same thing. Light can be thought of either as a stream of waves (light rays) or a beam of particles (called photons). Gravity can also be thought of as waves (gravitational waves) or particles (gravitons).

light ray

photon

GRAVITY THE WEAKLING

Gravity is the weakest by far of the four fundamental forces. It is around 10 thousand trillion, trillion, trillion (10 followed by 40 zeros) times weaker than the electromagnetic force responsible for light.

LOOKING FOR GRAVITY

Gravitational wave telescopes are not much like ordinary telescopes. The first one, built in 1970 at the University of Maryland, was a massive aluminum can that weighed about 5 tons (4.5 tonnes). Today's researchers use gravitational wave detectors called laser interferometers (below). These are based on two laser beams that meet one another. If gravitational waves are present, they disturb one of the beams. This changes the way the laser beams interfere with one another in a way that researchers can detect.

invisible gravitons bouncing back and forth through space between them. Gravitons can also be thought of as a beam of gravitational waves.

Although gravity acts over an infinite distance, it is a very weak force. This makes gravitational waves extremely difficult to detect, and no one has yet managed to observe them. Nevertheless, the general theory of relativity predicts that gravitational waves are given off by massive objects such as black holes, so astronomers around the world continue to search for them using special telescopes.

All in all, gravity seems much more complex than used to be thought. A lot has changed since Aristotle taught the ancient Greeks—incorrectly—that heavy objects fall faster than light ones.

Many scientists, from Ptolemy to Copernicus and from Newton to Einstein, have tried to unravel the mysteries of gravity since then. Physicists such as Stephen Hawking seem tantalizingly close to unlocking the ultimate secrets of the universe. Yet tomorrow, someone could make a new discovery that could change our ideas of gravity completely.

WAS EINSTEIN WRONG?

The new International Space Station (artist's impression below) will carry a range of extremely precise clocks to test Einstein's relativity theory. If gravity and motion affect the clocks as Einstein predicted, they will show different times from those on Earth. If not, this would suggest Einstein was wrong after all— and could lead to completely new theories of gravity. An earlier version of this experiment was done in 1971 (*see* page 27), which confirmed Einstein's special theory of relativity precisely. The new experiment will also test the general theory of relativity.

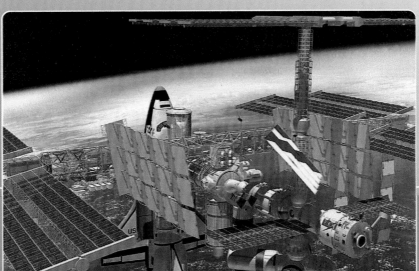

ON A ROLL!

An object that is raised above the ground has a kind of energy called gravitational potential energy. When it is allowed to fall this is converted to kinetic energy.

GOALS
1. Change potential energy into kinetic energy.
2. Find out how the distribution of weight affects the movement of a spinning object.

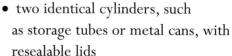

WHAT YOU WILL NEED

- two identical cylinders, such as storage tubes or metal cans, with resealable lids
- circular metal weights, such as coins or metal washers
- tape
- wooden board about 3 feet (1 m) long

1 Tape six weights to the curved inner surface of the first cylinder (not inside the lid or on the bottom). Put three weights under the rim at one end and the other three under the opposite rim.

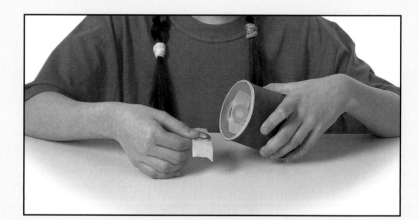

2 Tape a stack of 3 weights in the bottom of the second cylinder, right in the middle. It might help to tape the weights together first. Then tape another stack of 3 weights in the middle of the underside of the lid. Put the lids back on both cylinders.

3 Use books or bricks to prop up one end of the wooden board to about 1 foot (30 cm) high.

TROUBLESHOOTING

The cylinders run down the ramp too quickly to time. How can I slow them down?

Make the angle of the ramp shallower. The cylinders do not have to roll at top speed—you are only interested in how they gain speed in relation to each other. A shallower ramp will ensure that they roll more slowly and will give you more time to study the movement of each cylinder.

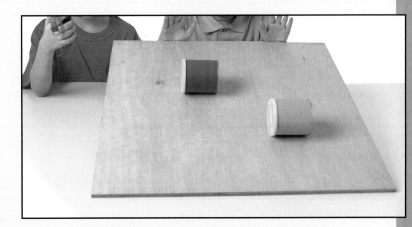

4 Try rolling the cylinders down the ramp. Figure out the best place to release them so they don't roll off the edge or bump into each other.

5 Now use a watch to time the cylinders as they roll down the ramp. Make sure they start from the same place, and don't push them—just let go of them.

TIMELINE

Atoms and Molecules	**2500** BCE Tin ore is smelted in Turkey **4th century** BCE Greek philosopher Democritus believes the world is composed of tiny particles that cannot be divided	**1450** European metalworkers work out how to separate lead and silver ores
Electricity	**271** CE The compass is first used in China; it works by detecting Earth's magnetic field	**1180** The first reference to the magnetic compass in Western writing is in Alexander Neckam's *Concerning Natural Things (De Naturis Rerum)*
Evolution		
Genetics		
Geology	**500** BCE Xenophanes of Colphon (Greece) discovers that land can rise when he finds fossils of seashells on mountaintops	**1517** The Italian scientist Girolamo Fracastoro suggests that fossils are the remains of long-dead plants and animals
Gravity	**1450** BCE Egyptians devise a water clock, based on the principle of dripping water **330** BCE Aristotle believes that the Sun and planets orbit Earth	**1345** Dutch engineers use windmills to pump water out of areas that are being reclaimed from the sea
Light	**6000** BCE People in Italy make mirrors from a rock called obsidian **1361** BCE Chinese astronomers record a solar eclipse	**1021** Arab mathematician Alhazen writes about the refraction of light **1304** Theodoric of Freibourg, a German scientist, works out how rainbows form
Medicine	**2500** BCE Chinese doctors begin using a pain-killing technique called acupuncture **1550** BCE Egyptians are using about 700 drugs and medications	**365** Mechanical cranks are used to set broken bones in Greece **850** An Arab physician writes about eye disorders and treatments
Context	**c.3500** BCE The wheel is invented in Mesopotamia **2630** BCE Egyptians begin building the pyramids **776** BCE The first Olympic Games are held in Greece **117** CE Roman Empire reaches its greatest extent	**c.900** Mayan civilization in Mesoamerica collapses **1453** The Byzantine age comes to an end with the fall of Constantinople

5000 BCE   **300** CE

1709 A model hot-air balloon is made in Brazil
1714 Gabriel Fahrenheit constructs a mercury thermometer

1738 Daniel Bernoulli proposes a kinetic theory of gases
c.1787 French physicist Jacques Charles draws up Charles's Law of gas volumes

1701 Edmond Halley draws up a map of Earth's magnetic field
1729 Stephen Gray explains electrical conductors and insulators

1742 Benjamin Franklin demonstrates the electrical nature of lightning
1800 Alessandro Volta develops the voltaic pile electric battery

1807 Humphry Davy uses electrolysis to isolate potassium and sodium
1822 André-Marie Ampere works out the laws of the movement of electricity

1650 Irish archbishop James Ussher mistakenly calculates that Earth was created in 4004 BCE

1809 Lamarck wrongly states that characteristics acquired during life are inherited by offspring
1831–36 Charles Darwin on HMS *Beagle*

1760s Robert Bakewell improves farmstock by selectively breeding animals

1831 Robert Brown is the first scientist to describe a cell nucleus

1691 Naturalist John Ray believes fossils are ancient life-forms

1793 Mammoth remains are found in Siberian permafrost

1811 Schoolgirl Mary Anning discovers the first fossil ichthyosaur
1815 Eruption of Mount Tambora in Indonesia modifies climates worldwide

1609 Johannes Kepler draws up laws of planetary motion
c.1665 Isaac Newton formulates his law of gravity

1665 Robert Hooke proposes that light travels in waves
1671 Isaac Newton shows that a prism splits light into a spectrum

1811 William Wollaston invents the camera lucida
1839 Louis Daguerre invents a kind of photograph taken on metal plates

1628 Physician William Harvey explains the circulation of blood
1721 Smallpox inoculation is carried out in North America

1745 The French surgeon Jacques Daviel successfully removes a cataract from a patient's eye—the first time this has happened

1805 Japanese physician Seishu Hoanoka performs surgery with general anesthesia
1811 Charles Bell pioneers study of the nervous system

1630 English Puritans colonize Massachusetts Bay
1665 Bubonic plague kills one-fifth of London's population

1787 The United States Constitution is adopted
1789 The French Revolution begins with the storming of the Bastille

1803 The Louisiana Purchase doubles the size of the United States
1833 A law is passed in Britain to abolish slavery in the British Empire

1600
1730
1800
1850

TIMELINE

Atoms and Molecules	**1892** James Dewar invents the vacuum bottle **1896** Henri Becquerel discovers radioactivity **1897** Physicist J.J. Thompson is the first person to identify electrons	**1905** Albert Einstein publishes his special theory of relativity **1910** The existence of the nucleus of an atom is proven by Ernest Rutherford
Electricity	**1877** American engineer Thomas Edison invents the phonograph **1885** American electrical engineer William Stanley makes the first transformer	**1923** John Logie Baird makes a type of television
Evolution	**1856** Male Neanderthal skeleton found; it differs in important ways from modern human skeletons **1859** Charles Darwin publishes *On the Origin of Species*, arguing his case for evolution	**1908** Marcellin Boule reconstructs a skeleton of a Neanderthal person **1938** A coelanth "living fossil" is found in the ocean off the South African coast
Genetics	**1865** Gregor Mendel, an Austrian monk, puts forward his laws of inheritance; they are published the following year	**1909** Danish botanist Wilhelm Johannsen defines a gene **1913** Chromosome mapping is pioneered by Alfred Sturtevant
Geology	**1861** The first fossil *Archaeopteryx* is found **1883** Mount Krakatoa, in Indonesia, erupts; it is one of the largest volcanic eruptions in recorded history	**1913** Earth's age is calculated at 4.6 billion years by geologist Arthur Holmes **1935** Richter scale proposed to measure earthquake intensity
Gravity	**1851** Léon Foucault builds a pendulum (Foucault's pendulum) that shows Earth's rotation. **1891** John Poynting, an English physicist, works out the value of the gravitational constant	**1927** Georges Lemaitre suggests the universe originated with a "big bang"
Light	**1877** Joseph Swan, an English physicist, develops the first electric light bulb **1882** Albert Michelson calculates the speed of light to within 0.02 percent of the correct value	**1905** Albert Einstein publishes his special theory of relativity **1935** Transparency film invented by American amateur photographers
Medicine	**1885** Louis Pasteur manufactures a rabies vaccine **1898** The cause of malaria, the protozoa *Plasmodium*, is discovered by physician Ronald Ross **1903** X-rays first used to treat cancerous tumors	**1929** Hormone estrogen first isolated **1934** Radio waves used to treat cancer **1943** Kidney dialysis machine built by Willem Kolff
Context	**1861–1865** American Civil War **1876** The Sioux Army of Sitting Bull defeats U.S. forces at the Battle of Little Bighorn **1897** The Klondike Gold Rush begins	**1901** Guglielmo Marconi makes the first transatlantic radio broadcast **1914–1918** World War I **1939–1945** World War II

1850   **1900**

1952 The first hydrogen bomb is exploded on an atoll in the central Pacific
1960 First optical identification of a quasar
1967 Domestic microwave ovens are sold in U.S.

1994 American scientists discover a subatomic particle that they call the top quark
2004 A "supersolid" is discovered by American scientists—it flows through another material without friction

1961 The first silicon chips are manufactured
1962 The first national live TV broadcast, a speech by President Truman in San Francisco
1975 First commercial personal computers sold

1990 Work begins on developing the World Wide Web
2007 American scientists create flexible batteries by weaving microscopic tubes of carbon into paper

1960 Remains of human ancestor *Homo habilis* discovered in Tanzania
1983 Fossils of a 16-million-year-old ancestor of humans are found by Meave Leakey in Africa

1993 The oldest-known human ancestor, *Ardipithecus ramidus*, is discovered by Berkeley scientists
2003 Footprints of an upright-walking human, who was alive 350,000 years ago, are found in Italy

1953 The structure of DNA is discovered by Francis Crick and James Watson
1959 Down syndrome discovered to be caused by an extra chromosome

1994 The first genetically modifed tomato is sold in the U.S.
1996 A sheep named Dolly is cloned in Edinburgh
1998 Human stem cells are grown in a laboratory
2000 Human genome is roughly mapped out

1977 Frozen body of a baby mammoth found in Siberian permafrost

1996 Signs of microscopic life are found in a meteorite that originated from Mars
1997 Fossils of *Protarchaeopteryx*, a birdlike reptile, are found
2000 The fossil remains of a dinosaur's heart are found

1957 The first satellites, Sputnik 1 and Sputnik 2, are sent into orbit around Earth by the Soviet Union
1969 Astronauts Armstrong and Aldrin "bounce" on the Moon's surface, showing that gravity is less there

1992 Scientists at the University of Pisa, Italy, make the most accurate calculation of the acceleration due to gravity

1955 Indian scientist Narinder Kapany invents optical fibers for carrying light long distances
1962 Light-emitting diode (LED) invented

1998 Lasers are first used by American dentists for drilling teeth
2005 Flashes of light are discovered to create X-rays

1950 Link between smoking and lung cancer found
1958 Ultrasound scans are introduced to examine unborn babies
1967 The first successful heart transplant

1983 The human immunodeficiency virus (HIV) is discovered
1987 The first heart-lung-liver transplant is carried out by a team of British surgeons
2000 Works begins on making the first artificial heart

1955–1975 Vietnam War
1968 Martin Luther King assassinated in Memphis
1969 Neil Armstrong and Buzz Aldrin are the first people to walk on the Moon's surface

1989 Communist regimes across Europe collapse
1997 Diana, Princess of Wales, killed in a car accident in Paris
2001 Attack on the World Trade Center in New York
2008 Barack Obama elected first African-American president of U.S.

1950   **1990**   **2010**

KEY PEOPLE

Aristotle (384–322 BCE)

Aristotle was born in Stagira, Greece, the son of a physician. When he was 17 he went to study at the Academy in Athens, which was then the greatest seat of learning in the world, before founding his own school, the Lyceum. Aristotle's writings spanned all branches of human knowledge, from zoology to politics and made a lasting impact on the thoughts and scientific discoveries of later civilizations. In *A History of Animals* and *On the Generation of Animals,* he described the characteristics of different animal species and attempted to explain their behavior.

Nicolaus Copernicus (1473–1543)

Born in what is now Poland, the youngest of four children, Copernicus had many interests. One of the chief among them was astronomy, and he spent many hours studying the night sky. Some of his observations made him doubt the accepted belief that Earth was the center of the universe. Shortly before his death, Copernicus published *On the Revolutions of the Celestial Spheres*, in which he argued that the Sun was the center of the universe.

Albert Einstein (1879–1955)

German-born Einstein was one of the greatest scientists of all time. He did not excel at school, but while he was working in the Bern Patent Office, Switzerland, he studied physics in his leisure time. In 1905 he published several important theories, including the now-famous special theory of relativity. In 1921 he was awarded the Nobel Prize for physics, especially for his discovery of the law of the photoelectric effect. This was to become a foundation stone of quantum theory in physics. Einstein was visiting the U.S. when Adolf Hitler came to power in Germany, and Einstein did not return to his home country, where he had been a professor at the Berlin Academy of Sciences. He later moved to, and worked at, Princeton University, New Jersey. On the eve of World War II he warned the U.S. government that Germany may be developing nuclear weapons and encouraged his newly adopted country to do the same. However, after the war, he and peace campaigner Bertrand Russell signed the Russell–Einstein Manifesto, which highlighted the dangers of humanity posed by nuclear weapons.

Galileo Galilei (1564–1642)

Albert Einstein described Galileo as the "father of modern science." Born in Pisa, Italy, Galileo studied medicine at the university there and later taught at the same institution. His many achievements included improving the quality of telescopes, discovering four of Jupiter's moons, and observing sunspots. He understood the concept of sound frequency and attempted to calculate the speed of light. Galileo also studied the speed and acceleration (due to gravity) of falling objects. He fell out with the Catholic Church over his support for heliocentrism, the idea that the Sun—not Earth—was at the center of the universe. This idea was considered to be heresy and he was placed under house arrest.

Edmond Halley (1656–1742)

Halley was an English astronomer and physicist best known for working out the orbit of the great comet which is named for him. He was fascinated by all aspects of gravity, especially Kepler's laws of planetary motion. Halley also established the link between atmospheric pressure and altitude, and worked out a method for calculating the distance between Earth and the Sun. In 1691 he built a diving bell submerged it deep under the waters of London's River Thames. And seven years later he led the first purely scientific voyage by a vessel of the English navy when he sailed to the South Atlantic.

Stephen Hawking (born 1942)

An English theoretical physicist, Hawking has done much to popularize science, writing a number of best-selling books. He has written extensively about the big bang origin of the universe and about quantum mechanics. His work on black holes in space led him to predict that they give off radiation, now called Hawking radiation. As a young man he developed a form of motor neurone disease, amyotrophic lateral sclerosis. His medical condition has worsened so he is almost completely paralyzed and can only communicate with the aid of a computer. However, he has lived for far longer than his physicians had forecast.

Robert Hooke (1635–1703)

Hooke was born on the Isle of Wight, England, and spent most of his life there, in Oxford, and in London. His contributions to physics included the law of elasticity (Hooke's Law) and his suggestion that light travels in waves. Hooke devoted much research time to astronomy and made many discoveries as a result of studying the night sky. He believed, correctly, in the attracting principle of gravitation, and that this force applied to all celestial bodies. He argued that the gravitational force decreased with distance and that in the absence of any such force objects will move in a straight line. Hooke corresponded regularly with Isaac Newton.

Edwin Hubble (1889–1953)

Hubble was born in Missouri and studied at the University of Chicago and Oxford University in England. He became one of the most influential astronomers of the 20th century. Among his many discoveries were confirming the existence of galaxies beyond our own, the Milky Way; and helping to show that the universe is expanding, evidence for the Big Bang theory. He was the first to use the giant Hale telescope at Mount Palomar Observatory. The powerful telescope that has orbited Earth at an altitude of 347 miles (559 km) since 1990—and which has provided much new information about outer space—was named for Hubble.

Johannes Kepler (1571–1630)

Born in Germany, Kepler was inspired by seeing a comet in the night sky at the age of six. He went on to become a great mathematician and astronomer. He studied planetary motion in great detail, and his published writings on the subject—his laws of planetary motion—formed one of the foundations of Isaac Newton's theory of universal gravitation. He became a supporter of the idea of a Sun-centered universe.

Isaac Newton (1643–1727)

Newton was an English physicist and mathematician. He was the greatest scientist of his era and one of the most influential in history. Newton became very interested in astronomy while at Cambridge University and eventually discovered that Earth's rotation caused it to bulge slightly at the equator and flatten at the poles. It was only in the 1960s that satellite photographs from space confirmed this. In 1687, with his friend Edmond Halley, Newton showed how a universal force—gravity—applies to all objects in the universe. His universal law of gravitation, first published in 1687, was first inspired—according to legend, by seeing an apple fall from a tree. However, it is not known whether this even actually took place.

Thales of Miletus (625–546 BCE)

The philosopher Thales was the first of the ancient Greeks to attempt to explain natural phenomena without reference to mythology. He advanced people's understanding of geometry, was the first to study electricity, and tried to work out the nature of matter.

GLOSSARY

acceleration A change in an object's speed.

alchemy A primitive science that sought to turn metals into gold and find the elixir of life.

astrology The idea that the movements of planets and stars can influence people's lives.

astronomy The study of space and the universe.

big bang The colossal explosion during which the universe is thought to have been created, 10 to 20 billion years ago.

black hole A dense concentration of matter, probably caused by the collapse of a star.

classical physics The physics of the simple, everyday world, described by Newton's laws.

comet A lump of ice and dust that moves through space. It has a central body and a long tail of dust and gas.

cosmology The study of the structure and origin of the universe, or cosmos.

eclipse An event in which one heavenly body prevents sunlight from reaching another.

electromagnetism The force responsible for both electricity and magnetism.

energy The property of an object that gives it the ability to do work.

equivalence The idea that the effects of gravity are the same as those of acceleration.

force A pushing or pulling action that causes a change in an object's motion.

galaxy A group of stars, dust, and gas loosely held together by gravity.

geocentric theory The historic idea that Earth is at the center of the universe and that the Sun and other planets revolve around it.

gravitational wave A type of wave that transmits gravity.

graviton A particle believed to transmit gravity.

gravity A pulling force between two masses.

heliocentric theory The idea that the Sun is at the center of the universe and the planets orbit around it.

interferometer A scientific instrument that makes measurements when two beams of light (or other) waves overlap.

mass A quantity of matter.

matter Anything that has mass and occupies space. Everything on Earth is made of matter.

orbit The path of a smaller body around a larger body, such as a satellite around a planet or a planet, such as Earth, around a star, such as the Sun.

perihelion The part of the orbit of a planet or comet where it passes closest to the Sun.

philosophy The use of thinking to study scientific and other problems.

photon A particle that carries light and other electromagnetic waves.

physics The science concerned with understanding mass, energy, motion, and force.

quantum mechanics A theory of how the particles inside atoms behave.

relativity theories The theories put forward by Einstein to explain space, time, and gravity, based on the ideas that the speed of light through empty space is the same for all observers, regardless of their motion.

space time A four-dimensional structure based on time and the three dimensions of space (height, width, and depth).

subatomic Being smaller than an atom.

supernova The explosion when a very large star "dies."

theory An idea that describes and explains something.

theory of everything A complete theory of physics that explains how the four fundamental forces work.

thought experiment An experiment conducted purely in someone's head.

universe All of space and everything in it.

FOR MORE INFORMATION

BOOKS

Anderson, Margaret. *Isaac Newton: The Greatest Scientist*. Berkeley Heights, NJ: Enslow, 2008.

Cheshire, Gerard. *Forces and Motion*. North Mankato, MN: Smart Apple Media, 2007.

Dreier, David. *Forces and Motion*. Chicago, IL: Heinemann Library, 2008.

Farndon, John. *From Ptolomy's Spheres to Dark Energy: Discussing the Universe*. Chicago, IL: Heinemann Library, 2007.

Jedicke, Peter. *Gravity and How it Works*. New York: Chelsea House, 2007.

Moore, Patrick, and Leif Robinson. *Astronomy Encyclopedia*. New York: Oxford University Press Children's Books, 2003.

Williams, Zella. *Experiments with Physical Sciences*. New York: PowerKids Press, 2007.

WEB SITES

Due to the changing nature of Internet links, Rosen Publishing has developed an online list of Web sites related to the subject of this book. This site is updated regularly. Please use this link to access the list:

http://www.rosenlinks.com/scipa/grav

INDEX